Inhabiting an Island

ISBN: 978-0-692-87578-0

Printed in the United States of America
First Printing: 2017
20 20 19 18 17   5 4 3 2 1

Cover photograph by Henrietta Reeve Bright. Copyright Henrietta Reeve Bright. Photograph used with express permission.
Book design by Ryan Scheife, Mayfly Design and tyepeset in the Whitman typeface

Apple Grove Press
P.O. box 413
Unionville, PA 19375

To order visit www.amazon.com or email StarrSCB@aol.com

Contents

Acknowledgments

I greatly appreciate the encouragement I received from my family and especially my friends who encouraged me to commit to writing poetry. Rick Benjamin, Sarah Corson, Barb Fernald, Gale Flynn, Sam King and Cathy Staples have all been instrumental in the creation of this chapbook.

THANK YOU.

Inhabiting an Island

Starr Cummin Bright

Henry's Jeep

At low tide wandering past rusted jetsam,
trap wire and lines, odd metal pieces,
I dream of repairing
Henry's Jeep
with these matching parts,
for who can easily let go of
such personal history?
Rugosa roses
now climbing through
the floor and in the driver's door
could entwine and bind
beach-combed finds for a new frame.
Wire mesh for traps could now be
a see-through floor.
Wild pea vines
would hold the gear box
in its rightful place
instead of resting on the back seat.
Woven grass mats
could cover the seats' springs
so once more,
Henry could drive the jeep,
rust and flowers
down the road.

Wind

All night the wind,
intense, intermittent
varied tones whirring
battering windows
slapping screens
whistling by eaves.
Uneven rhythm
tugs, disturbs,
rubs ears open
digs at dreams
nudges sleep away.
Clock checking starts
2:50, 3:30, 4:10, 4:40,
shut-eye ever more elusive.
As light mixes in,
scudding clouds
reinforce desire
to remain covered,
hidden,
absent from the day.
But the wind insistently
kicks sleep out.
There is no alternative
but to plant feet
and gird for bluster
that will buffet
knock me off balance
tangle hair

gust sand in my eyes.
My heart wants me
to be a turtle,
isolate, withdraw
avoid confrontation, conflict.
Whether it's words or wind
no matter how potent
the gale or tirade,
it's only harder in the end
to evade and mull
converse with myself
inside my own shell.

Laugh

Laugh.
Laugh unabated,
undeterred by looks,
raised eyebrows,
embarrassed smiles.
Whether dark humor
or straightforward glee,
laugh until your knees go weak,
your stomach muscles hurt,
so you lean on a bookcase
to keep from keeling over.
Laugh with abandon,
let those tears stream out of your eyes,
your whole body engaged,
quavering with mirth.
And even after you walk away,
shaking your head,
allow the after-laughs
to bubble up unexpected.
Why?

Life is hard

but
you can choose
your response.

Un-hearing

Three ospreys
weave overlapping circles
low over the lobstermen's wharf
replete with fish bait fragrance.
Their unmistakable broad wing span,
white belly, striped tail
have the mottling of immature birds,
that almost-adult,
but still-not-quite appearance.
A fourth flaps her wings
to maintain her place
high above the others.
She screams in bird tongue,
as a mother distraught.
Though birders say
ospreys always sound annoyed,
her anxious tone
strikes a chord with my own fretting
over teenage behavior.
I find relief somehow,
that the immature of other species
also delight in shortcuts to pleasure
ignoring the bird's eye view
of work for reward.

Some Guests

Mid-July:
just now first monarchs arrive
snacking, pollinating
the milkweed host.
July twenty-fourth, the milkweed's guests throng:
one moment settled, orange wings open,
next, chameleon-like, folded slits,
reflective undersides blending into
milkweeds' leaves,
dusky grey.

Warm sun draws out peppery aroma,
intensely heavy in the air,
inviting ever more butterflies
to pollinate, drink nectar, lay eggs,
so their larva will hatch,
and feed again,
like our recent guests
devouring meal after meal,
but with milkweed it's toxins -
shared from plant to larva to butterfly,
the adults now too distasteful
for most local birds.

Swells

On a smooth, windless ocean
under infinitely blue sky,
huge swells balloon from depths
raising my kayak on rounded peak,
then dropping us into trough
land no longer in sight.
As these swells of far off origins
freight into the shallows,
they transform to cresting waves,
roiling the pebbles,
so a roar echoes back.

The ancients would be saying
the gods of the ocean
are displeased:
floating garbage islands,
oil spills, decimated fish populations.

But at this moment,
in this kayak,
I am simply in awe
of the sea
so placid on the surface
while its powerful surge
grates the shore
eroding and displacing,
surge by surge
reclaiming its domain.

Delaminated

Coming apart,
not just at the seams
but the entire fabric.
The exterior hull
dried and cracked,
lies detached,
a fragile husk.

Tacking and brads
pulled away by the force of contraction.
Every makeshift method
you tried to use
to keep up appearances –
Gone.

The epoxy itself,
that skin-binding glue,
peels in the sun,
brown and flaked.
What you thought
was holding it all together
had no substance
in the face of self-destruction.

The true interior,
the guts of being,
lies naked
for anyone who still cares
to pick up the pieces.

Marker

(in memory of my nephew Nathan, 1983-2007)

I bike home
and look for it daily:
a trophy he'd carted home
from Baker's Island,
a memory stone,
a rocket,
now
his cemetery marker.

A reminder of life
where lines between
ritual, obsession and craving blur,
of the need to keep walking
despite and because
of fighting addiction,
when resignation is easy
but surrender impossible,
and escaping daily drudgery
is loud, insistent.
How does one ask for help
to walk through the day,
when everyone has their
own day, own issues, own turmoil,
while pride rages against the idea
that you can't handle it
on your own?
Just a day

then another,
actually
a cascade of unending days,
overwhelming
from this angle.
So you turned back, for one last time,
whether you knew it or not.

Terns

Their bubbly chatter
cuts through the fog
so I know they've returned
from below the equator –
arctic and common terns.

Social, garrulous,
they hover mid-air,
white wings tipped with grey
canting against the wind,
then dive
straight into the water,
emerging with slippery herring
in orange beak.

Old friends,
birds and humans,
whom I see only
briefly each year
arrive at this shore
after lengthy migrations
to feed their souls
and their young,
before long journeys home.

Their voices
lodge in my ears
and remain
throughout the year.

Circumnavigation

Choose a day when high tide is near 6 am
and launch from Sand Beach at dawn,
paddling south through the Gut.
This counterclockwise direction will
lessen encounters with lobster boats,
shorten the duration of sun in your eyes,
while allowing easy views of the island's coast.
Follow the shore, gently rounding the island eastward,
leaving Weaver rock to starboard,
while on port the canted sunlight
illuminates the tips of trees.
Throughout this time on the water,
breathe the salt air deeply,
observe the cormorants running-on-water take-off,
note the quick disappearing dives of sea ducks
which surface many yards away,
watch for bobbing seal heads among lobster buoys
and listen for breaths of porpoises as they surface –
they will dive to eat and return again and again.

As you head east
be intent on delving the passage
between the old coast guard
and the rock-edged thrum cap.
Assess the rollers riding you in
against the surf surging from the East,
both meeting in the shallows
in conflicted crosshatch.

The reflected sun's gold band
may blind you to rocks knifing up
in the ebb of waves.
Be wary of the adrenaline rush
as you divine the right course.
On the final wave's surge,
just when you get clear sight,
decide which eddies exist from currents,
not from barely hidden shallows,
and then you can cross, West to East.

Once clear of the waves
breaking on rocks to port,
observe other boats on the horizon,
some so far away that without perspective
they appear miniscule.
As you paddle along the north shore
avoid staring at the inland reef where
the siren-like breakers are enticing;
those cresting waves could swamp your boat.
Instead keep your eye on Marsh Head
and look for the osprey nest in the tall spruce trees.
The marsh itself is barely navigable,
noisy at this hour from the birds
during morning feed.
Straight before you
the mountains of Acadia Park
sweep up from sea level
providing a feast for your eyes.
When you come to Bunker Neck,
listen carefully before you round the ledge:

lobstermen can't see you
since now they have the sun in their eyes
and you don't want to be caught by sharp wake
with no sea for maneuver.

You will find the outgoing tide
creates strong currents in Gilley Thorofare
so hug the shoreline
as close as seaweed and rocks allow;
Near Hadlock Point
you will find the most great blue herons
ospreys and eagles
all fishing in their own way.
As you re-enter the harbor,
the sounds of the waking town will reach you.
Though the lobstermen will have all departed,
the ferry may be threading its way between
moored boats.
Pass the cluster of docks,
steering back to your start
to haul out the kayak.

Carry your encounter
with island and sea
as ballast for your day.

Seal Talk

Their tones flow up and down
as wind currents
howl through a crevice
rich with deep undertones.
Not moans, roars or barks,
more like caterwauls,
this eerie parlance of seals.

I hear the calls first as argument,
then as lament, perhaps with sexual innuendo,
and then as bickering, pushy conversation.
But when I paddle closer to their rocks,
they silence, slip off
and are gone.

I cannot comprehend seal talk
any more than I can handle
slicing dismissals or adamant truths
spoken by some people.
I want to slide off and submerge,
slip out of sight so subtly,
that they barely remember I was there
in plain sight moments ago,
basking on rocks in the sun.

Lament for the 10 B's

Years before I rowed as rehab,
before the terrier and I
(in my ninth month) rowed daily
while I thought of birthing at sea,
well before the seal played pop-up
first on starboard then on port,
perhaps before I could even walk,
this tiny flat-bottomed skiff
ferried ten children
to and from moorings,
idled with shipped oars for fishing,
and sometimes a strapping youth
would row her 'round the island,
gone for hours.

Once Rick painted
ten bees on her stern,
one for each child,
but by my time
annual coats of white paint,
which admittedly reduced leaks,
had obliterated name and art.
In fact, when I filed her missing
on the phone with the Coast Guard
I could hear the responder
click his teeth –
No serial number? No name? No registration?

We inherited this wooden piece of history,
alive as if a pet.
I cringe at being the keeper
when she disappeared.
Perhaps she's out on the ocean
roaming freely
and will someday wander home.

10 B's

(home again)

Shiny white paint,
inside, outside, all white,
screamingly white,
a blank stern
tabula rasa
though the family joke,
the 10 B's for the 10 kids
she had
not even twenty years first to last.

A floating island,
flat bottomed skiff,
glinting in the sun,
pearling the spray drops,
donations from the sea.

Oars shipped,
float and drift,
slap, thwish of waves,
tide and breeze the masters here.

Bounce, bob, rock,
pitch, crest, dip.
If I lie down and let go,
where to?

Fish Trap

A shadow in the dense pre-dawn water
turns into a flash of silver, as the fish slew sideways
suddenly visible as black speckled blue-backs
swarming en masse away from the push of the rising net.
The water roils:
heads, tails and bursts of swishy splashes.
As the net tightens, they rise to the surface,
blue green silver flying, darting in panic,
fear-driven search for an exit.
We gather them up;
the splash of salt water and scales
drenches my squint-eyed face
while their tail-thrashing sounds loud
against the noise-deadening fog.
As trays fill, fish pour over the edges,
they beat their tails against our rubber boots,
all-out efforts to return to the sea.
The filling skiff lists to the incoming side
where we lean out, netting them from the trap.
The catch complete, we steer back to the wharf
knee deep in mackerel,
their final tattoo thrumming the aluminum hull.

Muskeg

(Marsh formed by deposits of thick layers of decaying vegetable matter)

I heard it for years,
a sinister sound
as if departing salt water
were removing
life-giving force,
pulling marsh's muddy innards
to the surface,
an inward gasp
perhaps creating quicksand,
a quagmire shifting with the tide,
luring the unsuspecting,
those curious, into its midst,
only for them to be sucked down,
joining decaying vegetation,
adding bubbles to that
inward kiss of the bog.

Today I stood by muskeg's edge,
musing in the blowing fog,
when I saw a sharp-tailed sparrow
as it flushed from hiding
in thick marsh grass,
its strange call
illuminated the divide
between my imagining
and reality.

Imbalanced

My first time in a double kayak
with a man easily twice my weight,
he a beginner in the stern
I with years in the forward seat,
his doctorate after toiling against odds,
unearned privileges paving my path –
such an abyss of unwritten history.
An urban university professor
a farm girl turned vet:
imbalanced,

yet

we paddled with ease in the cold blue ocean,
arced the boat by leaning in unison
turned with back paddle sweeps
and forward paddle swipes
finessed dock landings
and finally beached the kayak
with a series of purposeful even strokes
clearly able
to act as one
balanced
craft.

Ladies of the Sea

By summer time
56 degrees is
simply refreshing
inviting multiple dips,
dives below surface
and foot taps
as they float on their backs and touch toes.

Two married to lobstermen
two lobstering themselves
at least part-time,
their monthly plunge
began as a lark one warm October
fifteen years ago.

A bond among women who manage
insular living
by getting out,
testing surrounding waters,
aware of safety in numbers
from times when they dipped
with riptides tugging their feet.

They speak of winter
of no swims below 20,
of ice on the beach
that continues into the sea,
slippery on the way out.

Water less than 40 seems like it burns
but feels so good getting out
they laugh and laugh.

We commend

(In memory of Lil)

We commend this body…
to the earth,
dust to dust?
Or to the sea,
mineral to mineral?

I watched Lil
spend countless winters on this island
population dropping below 70,
isolated when storms and seas
cut off boat traffic,
whose husband lobstered solo
no accounting of him
until he came back in the door.
Lil, the matriarch drawing all ages through her doors
for comfort, recipes, gardening advice,
who found laughter in cracks and corners.
She requested her ashes
be scattered in that same sea
off Baker's Island.
So came the procession
of lobster boats
eleven bright blips
on the radars
in the fog.
She joined other strong women of the past
who counted island winters not years

emerging hopeful and resolute,
who also chose the sea.

Now plying the ocean,
I imagine all these spirits
meeting, mingling, intertwining
strands of their lives
to buoy us, the next generation,
boats rowing against currents
swept by the tide,
caught in rising squalls.
Gleanings of these women's wisdom
float to the surface:
dark patches warning of puffs,
white caps heralding storms,
reminding us to stay aware
of the sea underneath and the skies above.

Ethereals

Lil and I on upended buckets
strip currants off loaded branches
listening to distant mowers.
"Damn snails" she mutters.

As I dive into clear water
my father swims beside me
"Go for it" he mouths,
bubbles streaming behind us.

I weed purslane's succulent leaves
while Lucille kneels nearby
"You can add those to your salad"
she reminds me.

I am falling off my roan horse
and glimpse Orville on his grey
chuckling through dangled cigarette
"Get back on the one that dumps you."

Chuddie, white hair, white tee
waves from his breakfast table,
encouragement from the now-blank window,
"Put heart into your run."

Tendrils

Stacked 5 high, 8 deep and 3 across
geared up lobster traps
wait for the sea to warm,
wait for the run
towards shallow waters,
for whatever purpose exists
according to lobster instincts.

Meanwhile, opportunists
have found their niche.
Rather than compete
with other low-lying vegetation,
the blue vetch climbs vertically.
Sneaking curling tendrils
through vinyl-clad steel mesh,
its branches encircle the ballast,
its flowers bloom in the parlor.
The vine of the earth tugs the traps
into the landscape of the marsh.
Brute force does nothing;
only slow efforts extricate
one vine at a time.

I think of this scene at night
when nerve fibers pull at my spine,
prompting distortion of muscles
once stitched to serve as protection.
No sudden movements,

only slow efforts each morning,
one stretch at a time
until standing upright,
walk 'til there's no limp,
shift, budge, turn, step,
until I can flow
despite pain's tentacles.

At Dewpoint

This morning
we stood on the beach
low tide infiltrating,
smells of what the sea deserted,
while the invisible bell buoy
rolled gently,
struck softly,
its clang carried blindly
to this kelp-strewn shore.

No breeze ruffles the grey glass sea
as it merges into soggy air.
Your boat vanishes,
no horizon
nothing to aim towards,
no mark
of your departure,
nowhere to pin
absence.

Spinnakers

Colors
skim across the sea
blues and greens
red stripes
billowed triangles
hauling hulls as if
vessels' tonnage were
mere trailing sticks
of kites let loose
to soar.

I am watching
my children lofted
by invisible spinnakers
only they feel clearly.
They are pulled
onto their own trajectories
undaunted by
deviations demanded
by unseen currents,
sure that the winds
will eventually carry them
to working harbors.

Even if their goals slip sideways,
as gulls in strong winds
slew across the sky,
old choices

still teach of gusts
thermals and downdrafts,
readying them for
for the next lofting,
the new destination
on the horizon.

Theatre

The stage: an abandoned lobster car
The actors: my son and his friend
The props: invisible swords and longbows
The setting: medieval Europe
The plot: subject to change.

I watch from the kitchen un-noticed
sudsy water clinging to my hands
wishing I could capture on film
the scene before me:
these children transformed
by untethered imagination,
where visibility has no bearing
because anything could be real.
One moment laying siege,
arrows flying, catapults launching
the next defending their castle
swords beating back, oil pouring down.
After the assault, opponents join forces
and now bear their standards,
together triumphant.

Line Check

The caretaker said,
"The water is on,"
but nothing came out of the spigot.
So willing to do the work,
to look for loose joints
spraying pressured water,
I pull on knee-high black rubber boots
and delve through the bog,
hummock to hummock
with occasional slips into
opaque liquid mud.
I follow the black water line
two-inch diameter vulcanized rubber
as it threads under dipping spruce branches
wends beneath verdant ferns
over moss and rocks
through tall grass and bog bushes
between two houses
with barking dogs
to the pump house
only to discover the switch
had been thrown
to off,
the result of sharps words
between locals
which at this point is not the point
because I have enjoyed
a quiet conversation
with the marsh.

Foggy Run

In thick fog, dense just after dawn
I close the screen door
scattering fog drops.
A deep breath now to fit
into cool, water-laden air.
Within a hundred yards
wet bangs are flopping with each step,
droplets decorating eyebrows,
a running shower.
An internal song takes over.
Nothing matters,
except this step and the next,
always those two, never more,
nothing less,
lulling meditation.
Gone are lists that played me to sleep,
calls to make, plans to set -
only celebration
of being able to receive smells
salty ocean
pungent marsh
fresh spruce trees
all simultaneously and separately
present.

Rosa Rugosa

Pause, bend, sniff.
I leave my nose
buried in a beach rose
to catch the wave
of aroma.

A balloon of fragrance
overwhelms
the pre-existing,
short-circuiting
all other perception.
Scent-specific nerves
remind me:
we once relied on smell.

What a change
as my nose
acclimates:
tonal shifts
from sweet
to peppery,
from entirety
to subtle whiff
to just fugitive flavor.

Letting go of the most eloquent
is not a loss
but a bequest,

ready to be stirred
to the surface
in deep winter.

Grace Notes

In music these notes are smaller than the rest
but size has no bearing on value:
a Yellow Warbler, all of five inches,
can stop the six spinning wheels
which kept you awake for hours.

They're considered harmonically subservient
but wild bog irises
though single blossoms on slender stalks
dominate both landscape and mind
with their simple violet elegance.

"Outside the rhythm"
doesn't dismiss the joy of dropping
everything to listen to a friend who appears
just when you need that bond
to carry you over the rough patch.

Musical ornament?
As if such embellishment were inessential!
Rugosa roses are decorative
but breathing deeply in their midst
is more like breathing hope.

Inhabiting an Island

Starr Cummin Bright graduated from Yale University (B.A., Classics) and became a veterinarian (University of Pennsylvania, V.M.D.). After being assaulted with a gun, she had to make career and life changes. She switched back to liberal arts skills and found a love of writing both non-fiction in her work as a business manager and in poetry. Starr had been visiting Little Cranberry Island, Maine, since marrying into a family that lived there year round and soon became deeply involved in the island community. Whether writing about the islanders she admires (there are many), of children growing up during the summers, of the birds and seals and fish and their environment, Starr finds many metaphors for life on this tiny island and the surrounding seas.